George P Carr

The Contest

A Poem

George P Carr

The Contest
A Poem

ISBN/EAN: 9783744709965

Printed in Europe, USA, Canada, Australia, Japan

Cover: Foto ©Thomas Meinert / pixelio.de

More available books at **www.hansebooks.com**

THE CONTEST:

A POEM.

---・・---

By GEORGE P. CARR.

---・・---

CHICAGO:
P. L. HANSCOM, Publisher.
1866.

To EUGENE A. CARR,

... eneral **United States** Volunteers, and Brevet **Colonel**
5th **United** **States** Cavalry, this **volume** *is*
respectfully dedicated by · ·

THE AUTHOR.

THE CONTEST.

CANTO FIRST.

I.

Goddess of ancient fame! Thou who did'st teach
Thine infant Orpheus the enchanting strains,
Which, penetrating rocks and trees, did reach
Their inmost parts, and breathed thro' their dull veins
The force of motion! Still thy power maintains,
Unharmed, undimmed by age, its former sway
O'er human hearts, and thy blest influence reigns,
The ills of earth and fortune to allay,
And breathe the power of song thro' our aspiring
clay.

II.

Child of Mnemosyne! Thy footsteps roam
Far from thy place of birth. Let not thy feet
Tread the bright vales that guard thy native home,
Till all earth's conquered nations shall complete
The grandeur of thy triumph. Sad and sweet
Thy numbers wak'd the vales of Italy ;
And Albion's sons with song thy coming greet ;
Wilt thou not, too, Columbia's patron be,
And cheer with thy glad songs the land of Liberty ?

III.

We offer thee a land of fruits and flowers,
Of hills, vales, mountains, forests, lakes, and streams,
And birds of beauty, in elysian bowers,
Shall sing thee to sweet slumber, and thy dreams
Shall bring from thoughts' dark caves the gems
        whose gleams
Are brightest, and from gardens of the past
Cull rarest flowers: the while thy future beams
Crowned with bright laurels, and the formless vast
Changed at thy touch, shall be in shapes of beauty
        cast.

IV.

I sing the man, who, in this latter time,
Rivalled the virtues of an earlier age:
Abraham Lincoln, and his deeds sublime,
Shall stand emblazoned upon history's page,
With earth's most mighty heroes. He to wage
War for a nation's safety was foredoomed,
And gave his life an offering, to assuage
The wrath of Heaven. While now he lies entombed,
Shrouded 'neath Fate's dark veil, the nation sits
    engloomed.

V.

Born in the Western wilds, his early life
Was passed 'mid scenes of rural industry;
His youth, ambitious, joined the arduous strife
Where heroes seek the wreaths of victory:
His manhood dared the slippery paths to try
Where Fame's proud vot'ries seek her temple high,
And gained its portals: thence triumphantly
His name, on Death's dark wings, soared to the sky,
And shines a planet fixed, whose brilliance shall not
    die.

VI.

Called to the Chair of State when treason's seed,
Sprung from the fruitful soil in blades of steel,
Threatened the nation's life ; he was decreed
By God, and by a nation's stern appeal,
T' uproot the noxious weeds, and to reveal
Her growth, triumphant o'er the deadly shade
Threatening to hide her lovely form. **His heel**
Crushed the foul serpent, and, **by Heaven's aid,**
His power the storms of war in gentle peace allayed.

VII.

His was the genius, his the **cunning art**
That raised the vast machinery of war,
And, when completed in its every part,
Made the grand structure his triumphal car
To ride to victory. He hurled afar
The swift avenging bolt, whose deadly blow
Blasted the upas tree. He was the star
Who ruled men's destinies, and, to and fro,
The puppets of his will, his chieftains come and
    go.

VIII.

As Jove, enthroned upon Olympus high,
Rules the obedient heavens in majesty,
Calm and unruffled, while the lower sky,
Moaning in pain, and tossing fretfully,
Gives birth to Tempest, child o' th' wind; so he
Guided war's storms; as calm, when, by their hoarse
And taunting voices vexed, the hostile sea
Threatened to whelm the Capitol by its force,
As when, abashed in fear, it rolled its backward
    course.

IX.

Though not apparent in each shifting scene
That marks the play, he was the guiding star
Of war's wide theatre. Calm and serene,
Mid all war's changing scenes; near and afar,
He ruled its destinies: his fame to mar,
Inspired the hope of treason's every blow:
His death closed the dark drama of the war,
And sorrowing millions mourn, with heartfelt woe,
The hero whose high worth his Godlike actions
    show.

X.

I sing the chiefs who at his high behest,
Leaving the soft delights of luxury,
Gathered from North and South, from **East and West**,
Their loyal legions and by land and sea,
Guided their way to **glorious victory**,
Or to heroic death.   Many a field
Well fought attests their skill and bravery
More forcibly than words, and they revealed
The power which Freedom's arm in danger's hour
      can wield.

XI.

I sing the noble sons of honest toil,
The men of sturdy frame and sweaty brow,
And the proud masters of a fruitful soil,
Who left the bench, the anvil, and the plow,
And with **a courage** danger could not cow,
Went forth to fight for truth and liberty ;
Free sons of patriot sires, they might not bow
Before the **traitor's** armed power, nor **be**
Ruled by their haughty foes, the lords of slavery.

XII.

Some rest in the bright " land of sun and flowers,"
Some 'neath the ocean's wave serenely sleep,
Some drag in torturing pain life's lengthening hours
Shattered and maimed, and some, more happy, reap
In pride their well-won honors. Let us weep
The dead and praise the living. Though their
  · names.
Who died are lost, nor flaunting histories keep
Their fame who live, their noble daring claims
Our love and admiration. They are fame's

XIII.

Noblest, and bravest children, for they fought
Not as the hero fights, who hopes for power,
Place and emoluments ; they were not bought
By stern ambition for a promised dower
Of honors and renown ; but in the hour
Of darkness and of danger they went forth,
And fearless braved the battle's leaden shower,
To prove the strength and courage of the North,
And save from trait'rous foes the country of their
    birth.

XIV.

Sumpter is fallen! On th' encircling **wires**,
Which gird the earth with tho't, the message stream'd,
By lightning borne, and in its subtle **fires**,
Far through the Northern sky defiant gleamed.
A flash! a pause! then **the report.** It seemed,
Not that the spark **was sent by** mortal hand;
But they **who** heard **the** message, might have deemed
A thunderbolt had fallen, at Heaven's command,
To rouse **to** ire and war the too long slumbering
    land.

XV.

Treason, for many a year, in halls of state,
Had shown his front unto the gaping crowd
Defiantly; and men who would be great,
Esponsed his dastard cause, with mouthings loud
Of feigned abuses. Slavery's minions proud,
Prated of liberty in speeches grand,
Until the rabble, by their speech endowed
With boldness, **raised** its parricidal hand
To strike with war and death our free **and happy**
    land.

XVI.

Then came the call "to arms;" and from the fields
Where plenteous stores the culturing hand await,
And from the busy shops where labor yields
The golden harvests which her servants sate,
From halls of science, and from halls of state,
From the bright homes where peaceful trade has
    shed
Her golden showers, the high, the low, the great,
Roused into action by the signal dread,
Marched to the field of war, with firm, unflinch-
    ing tread.

XVII.

Sons left their father's homes ; husbands their wives ;
Brothers from sisters did unkindly start,
And he, who owned the sacred flame which gives
A tinge of heaven to life's cold, venal mart,
Dared from the charms of life and love to part,
Laid as a sacrifice, with steady hand,
Th' uprooted tendrils of a bleeding heart
Upon the altar of his native land,
And took in her defense his sword and battle-brand.

XVIII.

One proud and brave in that devoted band,
A city's idol, and a nation's pride;
Was doomed to fall by the assasin's hand,
In the first flush of hope. His promised bride
Mourns the lost life so near with her's allied;
His comrades weep for him they loved so well;
His country owns his memory, far and wide,
With martial honors, and a funeral knell
Rung o'er the sorrowing land when gallant Ells-
      worth fell.

XIX.

As rivers, fed by the converging rills,
Each from its separate spring, its fountain head,
Themselves converging, leave their native hills,
And still increasing in their onward tread,
Seek the broad plains by all earth's waters fed,
Where hoary Neptune, 'neath the placid deep,
Reigns on his coral throne in splendor dread,
While faithful sentinels their vigils keep
Over the caverns dark where wind and tempest
      sleep:

XX.

So rushed the tide of men; and as the sea,
Tempest and wind let loose, in anger wide
Riseth sublime, and dasheth fretfully
Against the shores, with wind and wave allied
Threat'ning destruction; **so the living tide,**
Swayed by the gusts of passion, which so high
Can raise the human soul, that in its pride
It scorneth death and danger, rushed to try
Its prowess 'gainst the foe, and vengeance was the
  cry.

XXI.

And as old Neptune, in his marble halls
Lying at ease reclined, with lordly mien,
Calm, and unruffled, sendeth and recalls
The sprites who vent in awful storms his spleen
Upon the upper waves, his realms serene;
So Truth, the heavenly angel who presides
O'er the world's destinies, sitteth unseen,
Ruling for her own ends the stormy tides
Of human passion, and her time in silence bides.

XXII.

Oh Truth !   Bright offspring of the **Infinite !**
Angel most radiant of th' immortal band !
Clothed in celestial beauty, thou dost sit,
Guiding the loom which weave's time's woof fore-
          planned
Into th' infinite warp, with thine own **hand ;**
Charmed, meanwhile, by music of the **spheres**
Rolling in harmony ; thy works shall stand
Gaining in brightness, through the blood, the tears,
And all **the sorrows dark** which **cloud the rolling**
          years.

XXIII.

Empires have fallen ; nations sunk in night,
And blighted races passed from earth away.
Thou call'st new governments, new realms **to light,**
Freed from the elements of their **decay,**
That they may better serve thine ends.   **Their sway,**
Improved by Reason and by Liberty,
Heralds the coming of thy brighter **day,**
And shadows forth the time when there shall be
A nobler **race of men, in soul, in body free.**

XXIV.

Doctrines, forms, systems pass away : but Truth
Still cheers with her glad form the human soul,
And bright in hues of everlasting youth,
Smiles with a beauty Fate may not control.
Her power increases as the ages roll
Their dying years into the buried past,
And when our age and race are but a scroll,
Her priests shall still unfold her myst'ries vast,
And worship at her shrine while earth and time
      shall last.

XXV.

And now, the mass with proper arms supplied,
And subdivided in its various bands,
Th' appointed leaders to their posts divide
To teach the art of war and its commands.
Stern discipline, although thy rough demands
Suit not lessons of our peaceful days,
He must be led by thine unerring hands,
Who 'mid the iron hail and cannon's blaze,
On death or victory unmoved would fix his gaze.

XXVI.

The army lay about the Capitol,
Gaining in strength and discipline each day ;
But still impatient, longing for the call,
Which to war's stirring scenes should guide its way :
It came heart-thrilling ; but, **ere he essay**
A forward move in force, the chief whose hand
On battle-field this cumbrous mass must sway,
Gathering the whole array in concourse grand,
In pomp of martial pride reviews his new command.

XXVII.

Grand are the scenes of earth :   Its boundless sea,
Dark caves, and mounts with misty summits **gray,**
Forests and plains which boundless seem to be,
Have each some separate grandeur to display ;
But grander far than these is the array
Of armed men, when bursting on the sight,
While the fifes scream, drums **beat, and trumpets**
        bray,
They march into the field, with banners bright,
The while their burnished arms reflect the morning
        light.

XXVIII.

So thought the chief, as o'er the living mass
He cast his eye, and took th' alloted stand
Upon the plain, where in his sight should pass
For his review the whole assembly grand;
The army stands in line: then, at command,
Quick wheeling into column passes by
The place where sits the chief. Each separate band
Seeks the proud favor of his haughty eye,
And longs in battle's strife its prowess good to try.

XXIX.

And it is beautiful: The band's array,
Whose music soothes the soldier's fond regrets,
The waving plumes, swords bright, and banners gay,
And prancing charger that impatient frets,
Have each their charm. The lines of bayonets
Pass by with steady tramp, and now appear
The well-trained "dogs of war," the general's
      pets,
The band, who, on the field where cowards fear,
Discourse the music sweet which warriors love to
      hear.

XXX.

But couldst thou look with the far-seeing eyes
Which through the mists of sense, with clearer light,
See the dark portent that reflected lies
Upon the picture from the future's night,
Thou wouldst not deem it beautiful.   Their sight
Reveals the gulf before that grand array ;
The grinning Death behind each banner bright ;
Above, the vulture waiting for his prey ;
Below, the graves where soon their bodies shall
    decay.

XXXI.

Seest thou yon brilliant youth in gay attire,
With golden locks, and cheeks as roses fair,
Where sit hope's radiant smiles ; checking the fire
Of the wild steed that owns his guiding care ?
Soon shall a youthful bride in sorrow wear
Mourning for him whose beauty could not save,
A mother weep for him in wild despair :
While choking grass, and noxious weeds shall wave
In rank luxuriance o'er his undiscovered grave.

XXXII.

And now the march begins: A well-trained band,
Courageous lead the advance, a chosen few :
Behind, in order by their leader planned,
The different arms of service.   Could thy view,
From some commanding point at once look through
In its full length and shape this various throng,
'Twould seem a serpent vast, of varied hue,
That from the coil unfolds its sinews strong,
And o'er th' unwilling earth " drags its slow length
      along."

XXXIII.

Days pass ! 'tis night ! and slumber rules the host
On earth's protecting bosom lying low, .
Save where the sentinel upon his post
Walks his unwelcome beat with footsteps slow,
Straining his sight for sign of lurking foe,
And thinks of home and friends : anon his eye
Discerns an object flitting to and fro
Amid the slumbering host.   Is it a spy ?
In vain its semblance strange he seeketh to descry.

XXXIV.

Spell bound he gazes, as with stealthy tread
It threads the slumbering host ; with what design ?
Sometimes erect, bending sometimes its head
Over a slumbering group, as 'twould divine
Their thoughts and characters. Tracing a sign
Of mystic meaning over one, it saith
A mystic word. And now 'twould cross his line.
" Halt !   Halt !"   A freezing chill that took   his
        breath,
It vanished from his sight.   It was the spectre
        Death,

XXXV.

Who, rambling o'er the field with purpose dark,
In that curst hour, with his all-blighting wand,
Upon his victims' brows had set his mark ;
That he in battle's hour might know the brand,
And take them to himself.   Who e're his hand
Has touched ; that touch the bound of life defines,
And for the members of that sleeping band
O'er whom his wand hath traced those mystic lines,
To-morrow's rising sun shall be the last that shines.

XXXVI.

Now, rising from his couch mid Orient hills,
The god of day in state begins his rounds,
The lark her morning song in rapture trills,
Soaring aloft toward th' ethereal bounds,
And drums beat loudly. Thrilling now resounds
The reveille ; and now the vast array
Is all astir. And now " the General " sounds,
And now " to arms " the brazen trumpets bray:
Now " forward " is the call, and now we are away

XXXVII.

Upon our onward march, and soon we pass,
At Sudley's well known ford, a lovely stream
Bordered by fields of waving grain. Alas !
Is there the soul so cowardly, could dream
Of death 'mid such a scene ? The sky's bright
    gleam,
The stream, air, birds, the herd whose tinkling bell
Sounds like the echoes of a fairy dream ;
A gleam of light ! A crash ! A screaming shell,
A sheet of flame and smoke, as though the depths
    of hell

XXXVIII.

Had yawned before us, showed us that the fray
Sought for so many days was now begun.
Burnside commands the advance, and takes his way,
Driving the rebel lines ; while Heintzlemann,
And Hunter hold the ground which he has won.
O'er Stonebridge, on the road from Warrenton
To Centreville, now rolls the war cloud dun,
And Sherman's guns upon the left, anon,
Are heard, the foe falls back, the field is almost
     won.

XXXIX.

New England's sons have bravely stormed the
    height
Where blackest lowers the battle's sable pall ;
But, from the pits and breastworks on their right,
The leaden showers their purposes forestall,
And, filing to the left, they backward fall
Slowly and stubborn.   An exulting cry
Bursts from the foe, as Smith, heeding their call
For help, upon the field they now descry,
With fresh, exultant troops our bleeding ranks to try.

XL.

Then came the shock of war: **As when the sea**
Rusheth impetuous 'gainst the firmest shores
In anger, and retiring stubbornly,
Again his backward tide in fury pours,
And baffled of his prey in madness roars;
So rushed the battle's tides. All thou canst call
Mortal seems passed away. The sight restores
Each man a rock, each rank a solid wall,
The foe, the tempest dark that threateneth its fall.

XLI.

Elzey and **Earley** massing **on our** right,
Mow down **our thinning** ranks, an easy prey,
And still, as fresh supports appear in sight
For them, and none for us, **we** backward **sway**
Slowly; **now** break; now flee in wild dismay,
Crushed, broken, overwhelmed. As when the tide,
Clearing each barrier in its onward way,
Spreads **the engulfing ruin far and** wide;
So the pursuing foe appears on every side.

XLII.

Where is the bright array which on the morn,
Burning with martial pride and courage high,
Began the fatal day ?   Their banners torn,
And trampled on; their arms thrown down ; they
     fly
Pallid with fear, and each excited eye
Suspicious sees th' avenging death concealed
Behind each rock, each tree ; each weight thrown by,
With straining limbs they shun the fatal field,
And 'gainst the dreaded foe their swiftness is their
     shield.

XLIII.

In vain McDowell seeks to check the rout,
And Heintzlemann to stem the ebbing tide ;
Tyler essays in vain, his sabre out,
To stop the fugitives.   Their martial pride,
Their discipline are gone.   Each threat defied,
Wretched they fly ; and mid the crash, the jar
Of struggling thousands, in disorder wide,
Upon the fields and roads, near and afar,
Wrecked and dismantled lie the implements of war.

XLIV.

But let us not forget before they fly,
E'er overpowered our legions backward sway,
The deeds of daring and of courage high,
Which, through the mists of that disastrous day,
Shine with a light whose brilliance doth allay
The darkness of its loss.   Many a brave
And true heart perished there.   Nor can we say
That they are lost whose valor could not save,
Their names shall stand redeemed triumphant o'er
        the grave.

XLV.

There perished Haggerty ; there Slocum fell ;
And there, cut down untimely, died Ballou ;
And thou brave Cameron : thy funeral knell
Shall shroud with gloom the Capitol, and bow
Its proudest heads in grief.   Much honored, thou
Hadst hoped a brilliant future.   But the grave
Knows no distinctions.   Nor the lordly brow,
Nor friends, nor rank, nor honors high can save
The fated bark of life from Death's allwhelming
        wave.

XLVI.

Sherman! Thou, too, wast there. Did thy proud soul
Share in the gloom which from that fatal field
Spread o'er the sorrowing land? Did its control
Make thee despondent? Or was there revealed
A forethought of the time when thou shouldst wield.
Victorious, freedom's sword? When, led by thee,
A conquering host, thy courage for its shield,
Should march triumphant to the sounding sea,
And plant upon its shores the banner of the free.

XLVII.

Who knows the moral of this dreadful day,
This halt in freedom's progress? What the harms,
The hidden springs, the causes deep that lay
Under its revelations dark. What charms
Weakened our strength, and paralyzed our arms?
Was't the foes strong battalions? No! Their power
Aided, but did not cause the dire alarms,
Which in the bud nipped the new opening flower
Of blooming victory in that disastrous hour.

XLVIII.

Oft times a spirit stirring in the air,
Th' unseen, but potent fear, whose dark wings flit
Over the battle-field, has brought despair
Unto the bravest hearts; its influence lit
Disastrous on our standards.   It was fit
We should be humbled, and our punishment
Was but our dues: on whom the Infinite
Hath laid his chastening rod, in reverence bent,
Let him adore His name, and of his sins repent.

XLIX.

Hard are the lessons of experience,
But wholesome in their teachings.   It was good
That we be humbled, thrown on our defense,
Menaced somewhat, that we might be endued
To know the full extent and magnitude
Of our allotted task.   The monster birth,
The armed men sprung of treason, are subdued
Not in a day; but desolate many a hearth
Must be, and war and flames must curse the shud-
    dering earth.

L.

We were too sure, too confident.   We hoped
The treason blatant, with whose firm array
Our Senators for thirty years had coped,
By arms to conquer in a single day,
And hugged the fatal error, till its sway
Had brought us nigh to ruin.   We were taught
That right not always wins in bloody fray;
That not by numbers great is victory bought;
But by stern discipline and battle wisely fought.

LI.

'Tis thus in all the varied scenes of life:
Trusting too much its native powers, the mind
Enters too soon upon earth's field of strife,
Exulting, ardent, hopeful, till we find
Defeat rewards us, and the soul confined,
And clipped her fancy's soaring wings, must bend
To years of patient toil, and be resigned
To walk awhile the earth, that in the end,
To truth's sublimest heaven, in pride she may
    ascend.

LII.

We stoop to conquer. Would thy daring soul
Ascend unharmed, ambition's loftiest height,
Or, by th' intricate paths of wisdom's scroll,
Seek the bright shrine of Truth's diviner light?
If thou wouldst leave, as impress of thy might,
New dynasties on earth; or if, more bold,
Wouldst be a guiding star in time's dark night,
Or pile in doubling heaps the glittering gold,
Ere thou control the prize, thyself must be controlled.

LIII.

As Jacob served for Rachael, thou must serve,
And if, when thou hadst done the task ordained,
The guerdon be denied, thou must not swerve,
But labor on until it be attained.
So shall it brighter seem, as thou hast gained
It through much toil and suffering, and when thou,
Toilworn and breathless, and, it may be, stained
With hostile blood, before Fame's shrine shalt bow,
With never-fading wreaths she shall bedeck thy
    brow.

LIV.

So he of old, who in his lonely cave
Passed youth's bright hours in tireless industry;
His friends, the rock, the mountain, and the wave,
And wrangled loud with the complaining sea,
Emerged the king of eloquence.   So he
Who hid from vulgar eyes the sacred fire
That burned within him, till its light should be
Brilliant and steadfast; when he touched the lyre,
Waked the deep echoing tones which mighty tho'ts
      inspire.

LV.

So Newton, toiling on through many years,
Evoked the power that doth the stars pervade;
And thus, thro' fire and blood, thro' groans and
      tears,
The all-subduing imp whom Mars obeyed,
Whose balls o'ertoppled nations, and whose blade
Carved in the flinty Alps his lasting name,
Maintained his onward march, till he had made
The world his suppliant; and in anger came
And stormed, and took by force the citadel of Fame.

LVI.

So he, our hero, daring to aspire
The highest rounds of fortune to essay,
Nurtured, unseen, the elevating fire
Whose light should lift him from his native clay
To be a people's idol, and to sway
The destinies of a nation.   To decree
The freedom of a race, and to display
The conquering power of hearts that dare be free,
Over the bolts, bars, scourge, and chains of slavery.

LVII.

So thou brave Johnson, who, in halls of state
Dost sway a power grander than kings e'er swayed,
Didst bear the stubborn will which conquers fate,
That priceless gem whose brilliance cannot fade,
Hid 'neath thy vestments, till its light displayed
Should make thee peer of princes ; more revered
Thus hidden, so displayed ; than hadst thou made
Its light vulgar and common, or hadst feared
To show its brilliance when thy country's need
        appeared.

LVIII.

'Tis night upon the battle-field. The stars
Treading the round of night's encircling zone,
Seem weeping through the fleecy mist that mars
Their native brilliance, and night's zephyrs lone
Chant a sad requiem, with fitful moan,
Over the dead and dying. Cheerless shines
On them th' unpitying moon: anon a groan
Tells human suffering near. The eye defines
Where many a manly form upon the earth reclines.

LIX.

The wrecks of the day's storm: bleeding, and torn,
And lacerated lies the form divine,
The image of its Maker. Is man born
To such disasters? Must the stars still shine
In future, as in past, on the red wine
Crushed from the press of passion? Has his crime
Deserved such punishment? Doth all combine
T' augment his misery? This truth sublime,
Shines thro' the lines of blood that mar the book
    of Time.

LX.

Man is but finite; truth is infinite;
Progressive he; but she for aye the same:
The temple she farshining from the height,
He but the pilgrim, who would write his name
Among her vot'ries, and, should foeman's aim
Obstruct his upward path; rather than give
The heights already gained, fearless his frame
Must risk the mortal combat: yea must strive
E'en to the bloody death; that they who yet shall
    live,

LXI.

Still pressing on toward the shining goal,
Gaining at length the glittering summit's height,
May drink from Truth's pure fountains, and the soul
May bask forever in the sacred light
That floods her palaces. Not lost the fight,
Though thou fall in th' ascent, thy closing eyes
See but the portals; but upon their sight
Who follow thee, shall break with glad surprise
Its inner glories, and the myst'ries of the skies.

LXII.

Nor art thou unrewarded : while our eyes
Weep sorrowing tears above thy mold'ring clay ;
Thy soul, escaping to its kindred skies,
Freed from earth's prison house, shall take its way
Thro' trackless fields of thought ; sublime shall sway
The hidden powers of wisdom, and its gaze
See chaos turned to shape by truth's bright ray ;
The while it tunes its notes of endless praise
To th' all-creative One, through everlasting days.

LXIII.

And though this earthly fabric may decay,
The victim doomed of death's destroying ire,
Its scattered particles shall still obey
The laws of nature.   Still shall they aspire,
Instinctive, toward the all-pervading fire,
That flashed its infinite glimpses on thine eyes,
And toward that truth, whose all-enchanting lyre
Echoed of hidden myst'ries ; till thou rise,
And take again thy course rejoicing toward the
      skies.

LXIV.

When, in the cycle of the centuries,
The elements which thy decay doth yield
To th'unthinking clod, again shall rise,
By life's pervading fires once more annealed ;
To their expanded sight shall be revealed
The truths, which in those centuries struggling
    thought
Has wrested from the infinite.   Concealed
No more, the things so eagerly now sought,
Common as "household words" shall everywhere
    be taught.

LXV.

Then shall a nobler race, with loftier powers,
More holy, worship at a brighter shrine,
Whose light, more fixed, concent'red more than ours,
Shall shine into the soul with more divine,
And clearer radiance ; nor shall creeds define
The color of its beams ; nor shall the sword
Tinge the priest's vestments, but his hands shall twine
The wreaths of friendship.   With a common word,
A common brotherhood shall praise a common Lord.

LXVI.

Next day the sympathizing skies in gloom
Wept pitying tears upon the sorrowing earth ;
Men trembling, told with pallid lips the doom
Of friends and comrades fallen, and a dearth
Of hope and confidence spread with the birth
Of the sad tidings.   Treason waved on high
His bloody sword ; while Freedom, sunk to earth,
Seemed struggling for her life, and Tyranny
Exultant clanked his chains, and laughed defiantly.

LXVII.

And still, as pass the days, the circling wires
Tell fresh distasers.   In the West, Lyon,
Too brave, has fallen, and his force retires,
By overwhelming numbers overthrown.
After a gallant conflict, Lexington
Is fallen, Belmont lost ; The air is rife
With rumors.   Baker, in the East, anon,
Daring the foe in an unequal strife,
O'erpowered, has lost at once, his army and his
     life.

LXVIII.

Lyon and Baker! Two more gallant names
Are not inscribed upon the glowing page
Of the world's history. Their valor shames
The daring high of the heroic age:
Years shall increase their fame: their acts engage
Undying honors. Conquerors o'er the grave
Triumphant they. At fate they cast the gage,
Bright as at dawn, their setting sun shall save
Their sacred mem'ries from oblivion's whelming
    wave.

LXIX.

Was he, the chief, despondent? No! his eye,
Prophetic, through the clouds of that dark day
Beheld the gleaming of the brighter sky
That lay beyond; when, by that fatal fray,
The humbled nation being taught to weigh
More certainly the purpose, and the power,
The hate, and venom, and the strong array
Of foemen; better from that penitent hour
Should rise triumphant and its foes should over-
    power.

LXX.

Trusting the workings of that sacred fire,
Which waked the flames of Freedom's dawning light,
And which, transmitted from each patriot sire
Unto each loyal son, now burns as bright,
As radiant as then.   He told aright
Our danger, and its cure; and made his call
For men to save the land.   They, for the right,
'Neath the Republic's standard ventured all,
Resolved to conquer, or in its defense to fall.

LXXI.

As Moses smote the gushing rock; so He
Opened the people's hearts, and they poured forth
Their choicest treasures, and unsparingly
Resolved on victory; the loyal North
Sent forth her sons to battle, pledged their worth,
To wage relentless war; each heart, each hand,
Nerved with a firm resolve that nought on earth
Should swerve them from the cause, till every band
Of foes should be o'erthrown, and saved their native
        land.

LXXII.

Saw ye the deadly foe of Liberty?
The bearded Lion? He, the beast of prey,
Who holds no man, who is, or dares be free,
In all the varied climes that own his sway.
The form crouched for the spring, the armed array
Of claws distended, and the eye intent;
But now, our cause triumphant, with dismay,
In slavish fear and adulation bent,
He licks the feet of her, whose form he would have
    rent.

LXXIII.

Yes haughty Albion, in thy friendships cold,
And purely selfish in thine every aim,
Lending to tyranny thy power and gold:
Though many fear, and all respect thy name;
But few can love thee, for, unto thy shame
Let it be spoken, thou hast used thy power
To crush, and not to raise. When Freedom came
To wed Columbia, thou gav'st for dower
Thy curse, and strewdst with shot and shell her
    bridal bower.

LXXIV.

And when, in later years, her form matured,
With death was threatened by the impious band
Of her rebellious sons, they were assured
Of thy firm friendship. Thou didst shake the hand
Red with its mother's gore. Willing thy land
Lent unto treason's cause its secret aid,
And when that cause triumphant seemed to stand,
And Freedom's bravest champions were dismayed,
In many a signal form thy gladness was displayed.

LXXV.

She hoped not for thy sympathy. Her cause
Finds not its advocates and lovers classed
Among the great of earth; but honor's laws
Might have taught some the gauntlet not to cast
Till a more fit occasion, for thou hast
Menaced her form when wounded, and in pain,
But rescued now she looks upon the past.
And if, indignant at her honors' stain,
She calls her sons to arms, she shall not call in
    vain.

LXXVI.

Let not the serpent dare the fatal sting;
Let not the eagle stoop to seize his prey:
Let not the lion try the deadly spring;
Let not the secret foes more base than they,
Exult in Freedom's suffering; though to-day,
She, rising from the earth, in faintness reels;
Victor, shall she the battle's sceptre sway?
And while a sacred wrath her pity steels,
Shall grind her foes to dust beneath her chariot
    wheels.

LXXVII.

To-day's dark clouds weep o'er a people bowed
In sorrow, 'neath a crushing weight of woes;
To-morrow's sun shall see a nation proud
In conscious strength go forth to meet her foes;
And the same wave that late receding rose,
A weight of anguish, o'er our troubled sea,
Advancing, shall, with front more bold, oppose
Its now augmented tide unsparingly
'Gainst Treason's bulwarks, and its force triumphant
    be.

CANTO SECOND.

I.

When our dread chieftain, in the dark'ning sky
Had seen the coming of the storm portrayed,
And heard from Sumter's walls the warning cry,
As the first gleam the gathering cloud displayed,
By vested power he summoned to his aid
The people's Congress, and its counterpoise,
The august Senate, which the States had made
The guardians of their honor, that their voice
In council might define the measures of their choice.

II.

They met when flags and banners flaunting gay
Throughout the happy land, and cannons' boom,
And martial music told the welcome day
Recurred, when the Republic from the womb
Of the dark past emerged, and from time's loom
Took the tri-colored robe of liberty,
And, clothed in beauty, went forth to assume
Her place among the nations, and to be
The savior of the oppressed, and guardian of the free.

III.

It should have been a day of mirth and gladness;
But the gay banners seemed to droop forlorn,
And the dark spirit of a coming sadness
Seemed on the pinions of the music borne ;
And the deep booming guns, that from the morn
'Till sunset told the tale of Freedom's birth,
Muttered a portent of the time, when torn
Those flags should be, and to the sorrowing earth
Those notes should tell the tale of many a desolate
     hearth.

IV.

When in due form the concourse was assembled,
Lincoln addressed them thus: "The time is come,
At whose prophetic shade our fathers trembled,
And which they sought t' avert. The fife and drum
Usurp the place of reason, and the hum
Of hostile bullets whispers to our ears
Th' traitor's serpent hiss. Will ye stand dumb?
Or seek to win by useless prayers and tears
Those who profane each shrine that memory en-
     dears?

V.

Ye are the bearers of the people's might,
The chosen guardians of their liberty;
Will ye surrender every sacred right
For which our fathers fought? and shall there be
No place of rest for him who would be free?
Shall impious hands destroy the happy home
Which freedom found beyond a dangerous sea,
And traitors rule in liberty's fair dome,
While through the scornful earth her exiled children
    roam?

VI.

In vain hath Freedom reared her sacred fane,
And built with careful hand its varied parts,
And placed its altars, if she have not lain
Its firm foundations in the people's hearts:
Else shall the demagogues' insidious arts
E'er long gain full possession of its walls,
And change its sacred vestibules to marts
Where at the price of souls the hammer falls,
And the scourge-tortured slave in vain for mercy
    calls.

VII.

The people are the source of strength : from them
We hold the tenure of our vested power.
What they approve, so we.   What they condemn,
We likewise must forbear, and in the hour
When o'er our sea the clouds of battle lower,
We hold the helm and rudder, they, the weight
Of rope, and mast, and spar ; that, mid the shower
Of shot and shell, unharmed, the Ship of State
Through battle's dangerous waves may bear its
     priceless freight.

VIII.

Ye are th' exponents of the people's will: from you
·Must come the action that their voice demands.
Ye, as their wishes guide you, must renew
Th' approval of our acts, and to our hands
Must give a force equal to that which stands
In arms opposed to us by land and sea,
And give the sacred seal to our commands
Of popular sanction, that our hands may be
Powerful to shield from harm their rights and
     liberty.

IX.

This is a contest for the people's rights:
Ambitious leaders seek to overthrow
A government whose chosen form unites
In equal liberties the high and low,
The rich and poor, and whose enactments know
No rank save that which honest merit gains
For its possessor, and where each may show
His native powers, uncurbed by custom's chains,
Whose weight in other lands the lowly-born restrains.

X.

A government which seeks the elevation,
And highest freedom of the human race;
To clear to all the paths of emulation;
To lift all artificial weights, and place
Each on an equal footing in the chase
For wealth and honors: Where the people weigh
Contending claims, and honor or abase
Whom they may choose; but reverently obey
Him whom their choice has raised their destinies to
      sway.

XI.

Such is the government, against whose life
A band of baffled traitors stand allied,
And seek to gain by war and civil strife,
The power the people's sacred voice denied :
Powerless to rule the whole, they would divide
The sacred heritage our fathers gave ;
Or, by its overthrow, spread far and wide
Their power and conquests; till, o'er freedom's grave,
Throughout our conquered land their serpent flag
    should wave.

XII.

By war this government our fathers founded :
By war maintained its power 'gainst foreign foes ;
And we, by treason's armed hosts surrounded,
By war must vindicate it, and oppose
The power which their embattled hosts disclose :
Those principles by force of arms maintain
For which our fathers fought, and, mid the woes
Of civil strife the traitor's hand restrain ;
E'en though our hearts best blood his murd'rous
    blade may stain.

XIII.

Let us, with firm reliance on that God
Who holds our fate in his all-powerful hand,
And by the stroke of his chastening rod
Corrects his chosen ones, and through the land
Exalt, or humble, whom his will hath planned
To honor or abase; with purpose pure,
Go forward with stout hearts, and fearless stand
The furnace blast of trial; being sure
That what his arm protects, forever shall endure.

XIV.

The assembly heard these hopeful words with pleas-
    ure,
And in accordance with his wish, decreed
That men should be enrolled, and food and treasure
Collected to supply their every need,
And gave its sanction to his every deed:
But some there were sullen and discontented,
Who with each word and action disagreed,
And, in despondent speeches loud, repented
That Union's broken band with blood should be
    cemented.

XV.

Foremost of these, Vallandigham arose,
" We hear," he said, " the battle from afar ;
But too soon shall we know the bitter woes
Of cruel strife and fratricidal war,
And, in the general crash, and hostile jar,
Who may escape unharmed?   We fly to arms,
And seek to bind to our triumphal car
Our captive brothers, who, by dire alarms
Oppressed, would guard their land from conquest's
     threatened harms.

XVI.

" By right of human laws and heaven's command,
Millions of human chattels bend the knee
To the proud rulers of their happy land,
Th' appointed guardians of their liberty,
Chosen by Heaven the instruments to be
Of their redemption ; but with impious hand,
Fanatics would destroy the sacred tree,
Whose patriarchal shade God's will hath planned,
A symbol of his power, through every age to stand.

XVII.

" And **strive with** wicked zeal, and without cause,
By argument, and by incentive speech,
To set those free, whom God and human laws
Have placed **in** bondage.   They would seek **to**
        preach
A word of disobedience, and to teach
Rebellion to the servant, and incite
In his obedient mind a wish to **reach**
Forbidden wisdom, and by treach'rous flight,
To seek the unholy shrine of freedom's baneful light.

XVIII.

" We give to Lincoln men and arms to **wage**
A fratricidal war.   Let us beware,
Lest, in the heat of conflict, he assuage
His hate by loosing from its sullen lair
The monster insurrection, and the air
Vibrate the shrieks of babes and women slain
By servile hands, and to **our eyes** the glare
Of blazing hamlets shall appeal in vain,
To save a shuddering land from terror's blighting
        reign.

XIX.

" And, when accustomed to these scenes of blood,
And strong in men and dictatorial power,
May not some Cæsar, of ambitious mood,
Found by the bondsmen's willing aid the tower
Of an imperial sway, and make the hour
That tells the subjugation of the foe,
The birth-hour of a tyrant, who shall lower
Alike on him and us, and overthrow
Our freedom, and no law save his own interest
    know ?

XX.

" Through the dim vista of the battle's smoke,
I see in future years a throne uprise,
Whose occupant with iron hand shall choke
Each breath of liberty. The tyrant's spies
Shall lurk in every home, and fraud, and lies,
Bring wealth and honors, and a servile horde,
Black as their lord's affections, shall chastise
Each word of freedom with th' uplifted sword,
And decked in power and gold obey his every
    word !

XXI.

"Let this fierce talk of war and discord cease:
Let hostile words and actions be suspended:
Let friendship, and the olive-branch of peace,
To our misguided brothers be extended,
With promises of full protection blended.
So shall they peaceful to the fold return:
So shall the government be best defended:
So shall the fires of discord cease to burn;
Nor the avenging sword brother 'gainst brother
    turn."

XXII.

Then, in the Senate, Breckenridge arose,
A noble type of Southern chivalry,
Whom for his eloquence Kentucky chose
Her champion in the war of words to be,
Which, 'twixt the advocates of slavery
And freedom, long had raged. Fit advocate
Of the select and chosen few was he
Whose ranks he honored. Skillful in debate,
And versed in ancient lore, in mind and learning
    great.

XXIII.

But in his every thought and action proud,
And haughty in his bearing :   Holding light
The praise or censure of the changing crowd
Whom he despised ; he kept alone in sight
The power, the interests, and the vested right
Of the patrician few, who held in chains
The laboring millions whom their craft and might
Had sunk in abject bondage, and whose gains,
Wrought 'neath th' uplifted lash, from the South's
    fruitful plains,

XXIV.

Enriched the haughty master who, at ease,
Enjoyed the products of their daily toil,
And in each changing mood, as he might please,
Scourged or embraced, and made the helpless spoil
Of lust or hatred.   To them nor the soil,
Nor laws, nor people of a foreign state,
Afforded an asylum that might foil
Pursuit and apprehension ; or abate
The punishment devised by a pursuer's hate :

XXV.

" Ye seek," he said, " to give th' approving seal
Of your most reverend wisdom, unto deeds
Begot of hatred, and fanatic zeal,
And **dark am**bition.   Having sown the seeds
Of civil strife, and discord, Lincoln needs
Your favor and assistance to fulfill
The destined purposes for which he leads
His armies forth, to conquer and to kill,
And shed the **blood of those who disobey his**
     will.

XXVI.

" **He** seeks your grave approval to make valid
His base **infractions** of the Constitution :
Having, against its prohibitions, rallied
An armed force to mete out retribution
To those who sought a peaceful dissolution,
He trusts in you, the odium to **efface**
Of damning **guilt ; and, by your base collusion,**
Hopes on the ruins **of** their arms to base
His power, and freedom give to a detested race.

XXVII.

" Can your approval confer sanctity

On acts of lawlessness and **usurpation?**

Or lawful make the action by which he,

Despite the Constitution's limitation

Of his high powers, decrees the subjugation

Of a free race, and seeks by force to bind

Unwilling states to a confederation

Whose laws they loathe and hate, and who com-
      bined,

By separation seek their sacred rights to find.

XXVIII.

" No ! let us rather say unto our brothers,

' Go ye in peace,' and unto him who seeks

By crafty argument to gain from others

The approval of his bloody deeds, and speaks

Of freedom while upon their heads he wreaks,

His malice and his lust of power, and strives

To gain a dictatorial sway, and ekes

Out, as his own, a nation's gold and lives,

While on our wasted strength his dark ambition
      thrives :

XXIX.

"'To him,' I say, 'mete out the punishment
Th' o'erflowing measure of his crime demands;
Restrain the will on blood and slaughter **bent**;
Nor give the men and arms into his hands,
Which in their cunning grasp shall be but wands
To raise, as if by magic, from the earth
A servile race, who, loosened from their bands,
Frenzied with rage, and drunk with brutal **mirth**,
To scenes of fire, and blood, **and** horror shall **give**
    birth.

XXX.

" Th' unauthorized increase of men and arms,
The reign of martial law, our ports blockaded,
Defenceless citizens for fancied harms,
Untried, by felon's punishments degraded,
Each right denied, each call for help evaded,
These base infractions of each vested right,
By any shade of justice yet unaided,
Portend the time when Freedom's waning light
Shall perish in the gloom of tyranny's dark night.

XXXI.

" But speech is all in vain: the time is come
When justice, law, and argument have run
Their course, and are no more. The fife and drum
Are heard instead : sword, bayonet and gun
Are ministers of freedom. I have done:
I only pray that in this bloody fight,
If gloriously lost, or basely won,
The hard won, priceless boon of private right
Survive the rabble's hate, and 'scape the tyrant's
        might."

XXXII.

From out the galleries loud applause resounded :
Then on the chamber such a silence fell,
As when a troop by unseen foes surrounded
Waits the arousing signal which shall tell
The fight begun, and break the powerful spell
Of unknown danger ; as, against their foes
Revealed, they rise, and boldly fight, and well ;
So from his seat the gallant Baker rose,
The traitorous harangue by reason to oppose.

XXXIII.

A man of powerful frame, whose silvery locks
The snows of many a winter's storms retained ;
He, in his manhood prime, had felt the shocks
Of struggling hosts, and in the contests gained
That martial fire and valor which remained
Within his aged veins :   These words he spoke,
In whose defence his life blood since has stained
Virginia's soil, when 'neath the traitor's stroke,
He found that peaceful rest, by war, nor discord
     broke.

XXXIV.

" Most ill, O Senators, would it become
One whom a free, a loyal people chose
To guard their rights and freedom, to be dumb,
When, in the nation's Capitol, her foes
Are vindicated and their friends oppose
Each measure to defend her sacred life
'Gainst their advancing arms, and from the woes
Of dissolution 'neath the traitor's knife,
Her sacred form to save by quick and manly strife.

XXXV.

" What had been said, if, in a government
Republican, in a more martial age,
A Roman Senator his speech had lent
Unto their aid who sought with hostile rage
His country's Capitol, resolved to wage
Relentless war, and raised his voice to mock
His country's **brave defenders, and assuage**
Their righteous anger?   From Tarpeia's rock
Headlong had he been hurled to meet the deadly
        shock.

XXXVI.

" **Ill fares it** with the land, when treason's voice
Sounds unrebuked within the sacred halls
Of government, and traitors may rejoice
Unmindful of the stern rebuke that falls
In the dark shade of those majestic walls,
From out whose classic niches in anger **frown,**
From the cold marble which their life enthrals,
The men of mighty power, and high renown,
Who formed this government, and sent it down

XXXVII.

" To us, their children, **as a heritage**
To be preserved and reverenced.   **Me, for one,**
Not the array of armies, nor **the rage**
Of hostile rabble backed by sword and gun ;
Nor all the embattled nations 'neath the sun ;
Nor apprehensive **treason's warning screams,**
Shall swerve from my allegiance, while run
Within these aged **veins** the circling streams
Whose every separate **drop with love** and reverence
       teems

XXXVIII.

" For that bright emblem of our liberty,
The sacred flag 'neath which our father's fought,
Which cheered their labors, as by land and sea,
From the life-melting fires of war they wrought
The fabric of **our** government, and taught
Submission to the tyrant.   Its bright stars
Shall still by pilgrims from afar be sought,
And to dishonored graves, and shameful scars
Its stripes shall welcome those who seek by civil
       wars

XXXIX.

" To mar its beauty.   When again its folds
Float o'er each city, and each wilderness
That owned their sway, and unto him who holds
Their standard, though alone and powerless,
Thousands of loving hearts and helping hands shall
      press ;
Or trait'rous hordes, sullen with secret hate,
Trembling in abject fear, his sway confess :
Then, and not till then, be it soon or late,
Shall our embattled hosts their onward march abate.

XL.

" 'Till then let countless armies tread the earth,
And whitening sails discolor the blue deep :
Let, until then, the people's lives and worth
Be at our chief's command ; that he may keep
Well-filled the ranks of workmen, who shall reap
This harvest of rebellion : Though the North
Be clothed in mourning, and the South may weep ;
Better the funeral pall, and desolate hearth,
Than a disgraceful peace with joy and festal mirth.

XLI.

Then, when the pæan of **our** victory
From ocean swells triumphant unto ocean,
Let him who bravely fought for Liberty
Seek the fair idol of his heart's devotion,
And whisper in her ear the fond emotion
That warms **his veins, and let the brave** dead **sleep**
Until their time; since death is but a potion,
Which he who drinketh but forgets to weep,
Nor bides from misspent youth **the ills** of age to
        reap."

XLII.

Then in the Senate Johnson **rose. A man**
Of powerful mind and fervid eloquence,
And fearless in his bearing, he began
His course at fortune's lowest round, and thence
By his own toil had gained the eminence
Of senatorial power. Since, he obtained
The nation's second post of **honor, whence,**
At Lincoln's death, the summit he attained,
And o'er a rescued land wisely and firmly reigned.

XLIII.

"A sacred impulse bids me rise," he said,
"To lift my voice in Freedom's holy cause,
And in the name of our illustrious dead,
To vindicate the government and laws
For which they fought, against his speech who
    draws
Pretext of danger from each measure taken
For their defense, and covets the applause
Of those who have her sheltering flag forsaken,
And seeks in loyal minds distrust and fear to 'waken.

XLIV.

"When Freedom, driven from Britania's isle,
Loosed her frail bark upon the ocean's foam,
From the cold tyrant's hate, and cunning guile,
Resolved, afar, to other lands to roam,
She found a place of refuge, and a home,
In fair Columbia's stately solitudes,
Built on its granite rocks her lasting dome,
And, 'mid its smiling vales and verdant woods,
Fixed on the fruitful soil her children's firm abodes."

XLV.

" A savage foe attacked her habitation,
Her children's arms his pride and power effaced,
The British Lion sought in exultation
Her new found home, and her fair form menaced
With ships and armies: conquered and disgraced,
His armies captives, and his arms a spoil,
Howling he fled across the watery waste
Back to his home, and left to honest toil,
Untaxed by tyranny, her rich and fruitful soil.

XLVI.

" And when a band of baffled demagogues,
Powerless to rule by right her fair domain,
Powerless to stop by governmental clogs
Th' advancing wheels of reason, or to'chain
The consciences of men, and to restrain
By fraud or force the onward march of thought,
Seek her destruction; shall she not maintain
·The freedom which by patriot blood was bought,
And shall not trait'rous foes her mighty power be
          taught ?

XLVII.

" This contest was not of the people's seeking,
They had no ills to cure, no wrongs to right;
But baffled demagogues, in vengeance wreaking
'Gainst Liberty their ineffectual spite,
Cheat their deluded victims by the sight
Of Freedom's robe, which hides the ghastly form
Of Tyranny, who leads them on to fight,
And we must fearless meet the trait'rous swarm,
Though at their deadly stings may flow the life blood
     warm.

XLVIII.

" This is a sacred contest: Treason rears
His hateful form and aims the deadly stroke
At that Republic, which, through the bright years
Since first her radiant form in gladness broke,
A shape of beauty, from the battles' smoke,
Has been a sacred refuge to th' oppressed
Of every clime and nation, and which woke
The flames of Liberty whose light has blest
Freedom in other lands by doubts and fears op-
     pressed.

XLIX.

" If, through our negligence, by force of arms
O'erthrown, she falls, she will not fall alone ;
But through the shuddering earth shall dire alarms
Seize freedom's champions, and at the groan
That tells her dissolution, every throne
Shall join to spurn her image from the earth,
Freedom no more throughout the world be known,
While at our vauntings of its sacred worth,
Statesmen and kings shall laugh in most unholy
    mirth.

L.

" But she shall never fall : though trait'rous hordes
Rise from the earth like locusts' fabled swarms :
Though unsheathed bayonets and naked swords
Gleam in each wood and glade, and leaden storms
Deluge the earth, the loyal blood which warms
The veins of sons begot of patriot sires
Knows not the fear of traitors, and our forms
Shall fearless brave the battle's wasting fires,
And comrades fill his place, who in the fight ex-
    pires :

LI.

" Till our victorious legions sweep from earth
Each vestige of the traitor's boasted power,
And show the government's inherent worth
To guard as well its rights in the dark hour
Of civil insurrection, as when lower
The clouds of foreign war, and to secure
To every sovereign State the promised dower
Of a free government, which shall endure
In earth's tyrannic night, a light steadfast and sure.

LII.

" Above war's lurid clouds and fitful flashes,
Where many a hearth and heart in ruin lies,
Like Phœnix, bright from the decaying ashes,
I see a great, a happy nation rise,
Governed by laws benevolent and wise
Which a free people reverently obey;
Where men of every race beneath the skies,
Each subject of contention cast away,
In common trust and love shall own a common
sway."

LIII.

The throng has passed away, and silence reigns
Where late the sound of loud debate was heard;
The spirit echo of the place maintains
Unbroken silence now, no longer stirred
To mock'ry by the ire-provoking word
Of question or reply.   A stern repose
Rests on the vacant halls, where late occurred
The clash of hostile factions, and arose
The windy war of words twixt firm but peaceful
        foes.

LIV.

In legislative halls no gory spots,
With tales of bloody death and horror fraught,
Offend the eye: no loathsome carrion rots
Whose once loved form by anxious friends is sought:
Yet in their lofty chambers have been fought
The nation's mightiest battles.   There have stood
Freedom's best champions, and they who wrought
The chains and manacles, and unsubdued,
Yearly have each with each the war of words
        renewed.

LV.

There dropped Calhoun his words of living fire:
There Clay's bright genius glowed with heat intense:
There Hayne sent forth his shafts of barbed ire:
There Webster hurled those bolts of eloquence
Fit for an injured people's strong defense:
There Douglas raised his voice in stern appeal:
There Jefferson displayed his power immense:
And there, with words like blades of polished steel,
Proud Randolph dealt the wounds which death alone
      could heal.

LVI.

They fought life's battle well, and died—but hark!
From out the mystic stillness of the walls,
From the dim recesses in shadow dark,
On the hushed air of the deserted halls
A solemn and unearthly whisper falls,
And moans, with cadence sad, " in vain," " in vain:"
Seek we the light: the spell no more enthralls,
'Twas but the fancy which a wandering brain
Caught from the moaning winds that sweep Ma-
      nassas' plain.

LVII.

No! it was not in vain, ye mighty dead:
Not vain your lives with wisdom's lessons fraught;
Not vain your deaths: the pilgrim's reverent tread
Sounds o'er the sole reward your fame hath bought,
An honored grave; but for our use ye wrought
A fruitful and a lasting heritage,
Oases in the boundless waste of thought,
Where the worn traveler of life's pilgrimage
His soul consuming thirst for wisdom may assuage.

LVIII.

And chiefly thou, whose honored ashes rest
In the proud soil of thine adopted State,
Thou noble offering of the queenly West
Upon the altar of relentless fate;
Not vain was thine existence: though the hate
Of demagogues would mar thy well-won fame,
Their dark'ning malice never can abate
The brightness of its lustre, and the name
Of Douglas, through all time, shall loving honors
    claim.

LIX.

The brain of mighty power, the eye of fire ;
The tongue sharp in attack, smooth in defense ;
The hand raised in appeal, or clenched in ire ;
Lips proud with conscious weight of evidence,
Or fiercely cynical with scorn intense ;
The firm-set brow, the citadel of thought :
The frame transfused with fervid eloquence :
The man from nature's best material wrought,
And in the school of toil life's noblest lessons
    taught,

LX.

Are senseless dust : The lake's complaining wave
Sings to the sorrowing shore thine endless dirge ;
But t'ward the precincts of thy silent grave,
Borne on the bosom of the billowy surge,
And on the iron bands which to its verge
Bind the wide regions of a continent,
A multitude of eager pilgrims urge
Their willing way, and there in sorrow bent
Gaze on thy place of rest, with love and reverence
    blent.

LXI.

And, though each vestige **of thy resting place**
Be swept from earth, and the unresting wave
Of time gulf, and obliterate each trace
Of the proud city of thy prouder grave;
The record **of thy** virtues still shall **save**
Thee from oblivion, and thou **shalt go down**
To **future times,** as he, who doubly brave,
Wore with mild dignity the victor's crown,
And, haughty in defeat, despised the rabbles' frown.

CANTO THIRD.

I.

'Tis sweet to sail upon the summer sea,
When skies are bright, and wind and wave at rest,
And sleeps the tempest.   It is sweet to be
Rocked by its motion to a dreamy rest,
And watch the rise and falling of its breast,
And think upon its myst'ries.   It is sweet
The depths with hidden wonders to invest,
And think upon the time when we shall meet
Once more upon the land, and anxious friends shall greet.

II.

So sang the sailors; as a gallant fleet,
Clearing the capes from Chesapeake's broad bay,
Its decks well-manned, its armament complete,
Stood out to sea, and bravely took its way
Majestic toward the South.   The breeze whose sway
Its sails must own, compel it bravely on,
The mariners with jokes and glees allay
The weight of passing hours; the morning sun
Cheers with his gladd'ning smile the journey well begun.

III.

Dupont commands the fleet: a man well skilled
To rule the sea in calm or tempest mood;
Born near its wave-washed shore, 'twas his to build
On the foundation of th' unstable flood
The temple of his honor, which has stood
Changeless amid its changes; his to roam
Its fields 'mid leaden hail, and showers of blood;
To pluck high honors from its fruitful foam,
And joy for many years in the glad harvest home.

IV.

Each vessel bears a hardy, well skilled crew
Deep learned in all the lore of sailor's craft,
Quick each command and motion to go through,
Or on forecastle, mid ships, or abaft
To gather at command, to build the raft
Or man the life-boat: or, while sad skies weep
In pity, to ascend the dizzy shaft,
And while the lightning's flash, and storm winds
　　　sweep,
To hang suspended high above the yawning deep.

v.

The fleet also in three divisions bears
The troops destined to operate on land :
Wright, Viele, Stevens, govern the affairs
Respectively of each.   The whole command
Devolves on Sherman : Nurtured 'mid the grand
But barren scenery of the island State,
He chose to follow o'er war's treach'rous sand
The beacon light of fame, rather than wait
For the slow honors which less daring souls might
      sate.

vi.

He, in the contest of the Floridas,
Had tracked the savage foe through wood and glade,
And, where the deadly contest hottest was,
Buena Vista saw his flashing blade
Dealing destruction, and he had displayed
In every post a skill and bravery
Which won him rank and honor, and had made
Lincoln to deem that he fit chief would be
T' assail a dangerous land beyond a dangerous sea.

VII.

And through the whole assemblage there was heard
The din of many voices ; cries and cheers
Come to us blended with commands' stern word.
Not much, I ween, freedom's brave soldier fears
Whom rank has placed above him : he reveres
His rank when duty bids, and danger's hour
Sees none in whom more readiness appears :
But he is all untaught to cringe and cower,
Or bend the servile knee to overbearing power.

VIII.

'Tis one of those bright days, when nature's fountain
Showers down new beauties from each sparkling
　　　stream ;
When earth, sea, plain, lake, forest, river, mountain,
And all the living forms with which they teem,
Suffused are with the pervading beam
Of that high orb, from which the love of God
Speaks unto earth, in the bright ray whose gleam
Warms as well the chill wave, and sluggish clod,
As the quick juice of plants, and living creature's
　　　blood.

IX.

A gentle sea with undulating motion
Like to the rise and falling of that breast,
Which no exciting care or deep emotion
Has fevered with the spirit of unrest,
Bears on the brooding barks, that make their nest
Amid its waving fields: spreading their light
Wings to the breeze, careless sail some: oppressed,
Others combat the waters with their might,
And pour forth lab'ring breath black as the shades
　　of night.

X.

As the climatic den'zens of the streams,
Warned by the voice of autumn's babbling wind,
Like the fair fabric of our midnight dreams
Mounting in air, and through its unconfined
Expanse seeking a clime where they may find
A more enduring refuge : as in strange,
And varied forms, and semblances combined,
About their dread and honored chief they range,
And at his high command in different orders change ;

XI.

So moves the fleet o'er ocean's blue expanse:
The flagship Wabash proudly leads the way;
And as the vessels on the smooth wave dance,
With light and airy motion they obey
Each varied call her signals may display,
Changing their order: from their coral caves
Neptune's fair daughters seek the concourse gay;
And follow it until Apollo laves
His streaming locks of gold in the far western waves.

XII.

'Tis night upon the waters! Darkness now,
Majestic, sits enthroned upon their wide,
Unlimited expanse, and the bright glow
Of stars reflected from the glassy tide,
Lights up the brooding mystery that would hide
Her grandeur and extent. The waves, with low,
Mysterious moanings sad, which seem allied
Unto the soul's fond yearnings, as they flow,
Pray Him whose mighty power the wind and tempest
        know.

XIII.

Dull is the mind, which, in such hallowed hour,
Soars not above the paltry things of earth,
Its loves, its hates, its gauds of place and power,
To think upon the infinite; the birth,
The life, and death of matter; of the worth
Of Deity, and littleness of men;
Of errors blighting sway, of wisdom's dearth,
And all the mighty myst'ries which have been
Hid since the birth of time from man's farreaching
      ken.

XIV.

Rending, at such a time, the veil of sense
That shuts it from the infinite, the soul
Enters its portals, and with confidence
Ponders its hidden myst'ries, and the scroll
That doth fate's problem intricate unroll,
Seems almost understood; but its return
Dispels th' illusion fair, and, to our dole,
Our dull clay hides the secret, and we yearn
In vain for the lost thought that never shall return.

X V.

And now a little band, gath'ring on deck,
Discourse in turn each venture that befalls
Upon the sea or land, of storm, and wreck,
Battles, and fires, and phantom ships; now calls
One for a song.   The lot is cast, and falls
Upon an aged seaman, one whose strong
But bended form, and hoary locks, the squalls
Of many years had weathered: Thus his song
He sung, the while the crew to hear around him
    throng :

1 " Oh ! a blithe old bark is this frame of ours,
As it sails on the ocean of years,
And breasts, in the pride of its varied powers,
Its billows of hopes and fears.
Blithely away, at the break of day,
It speeds from the misty shore,
And grandly it rides o'er the swelling tides,
To the sound of the ocean's roar;
But when, in the West, sinks the sun to rest,
And his ray gilds the horizon's verge,
Like a phantom of night, it sinks from sight,
And is lost in the boundless surge:

And whether it land on some far off strand,
Or sink in the depths below,
To eternal sleep, in the fathomless deep,
No mortal shall ever know.

2 " Oh ! a blithe old bark is this frame of ours,
When its masts and spars are tight,
And, impelled by the force of its hidden powers,
With motion airy and light,
It glides from the mists of the unknown past,
On the waves of life's changing sea,
And begins its course o'er its waters vast,
Dancing in mirth and glee.
Sometimes it rides on the placid tides
Calmly and tranquilly;
But anon the forms of the billowy storms
Cause it in fear to flee,
And when sets the sun, and the day is done,
And the night wind sounds its dirge,
Like a vision bright, it fades from sight,
And is lost in the boundless surge,
And whether it land on some far off strand,
Or sink to the depths below,
To unending sleep, in the fathomless deep,
No mortal shall ever know."

XVI.

Ceased the rude song, and now a rising cloud,
Escaping from the caverns of the deep,
Darkens the smiling heavens, and the crowd
Dispersing, seek their stations, some to sleep,
Others to watch. The darkening skies now weep
Tears for the coming storm, and now each sail
Is reefed, each crew now ready keep,
And wait their chief's command; he, calm, but pale,
Majestic walks the deck, and waits the coming
    gale.

XVII.

'Tis terrible to sail upon the sea,
When wind, and wave, and cloud, in fury clash
Against each other; terrible to be
Borne headlong on the billows, when they dash
Their crested heads to meet the lightning's flash,
And sink exhausted: terrible to be hurled
Down to the dark abyss, and hear the crash
When deep calls unto deep, and to be whirled,
A thing for the waves' sport, about the watery world.

XVIII.

Brave are the hearts that dare the stormy tide,
And worthy of all praise. Their bravery
Dares not alone the cannon's breath; allied,
The powers of earth, and air, of sea, and sky,
Compass for their destruction, and the high,
Shot-riding death has not the fatal power
That lurks in th' elements, the sea, and sky,
Are deadlier far, when clouds in anger lower,
Than storms of shot and shell in battle's fiery hour.

XIX.

Goldsborough, Farragut, Dupont, and Davis' names,
On hist'ry's page in golden words shall glow,
And go far down to future days, and fame's
Bright record pay the debt a people owe
Unto their brave defenders. Green shall grow
In loyal hearts brave Dahlgren's memory;
Worden and Ward not unrewarded go,
Porter! thy country drinks a health to thee,
And never fading, Wilkes! shall thy bright laurels
    be.

XX.

And thou brave **Foote!** whose character refined,
With martial valor Christian love enwove;
Bearing, 'mid all war's **storms,** a heart resigned
To do the holy will of One above,
Who doth as well the wind and waters move,
As man's wild passions: thou hast left a fame,
Which, on the wings of our endearing love
Rising triumphantly, shall make thy name
Bright as th' immortal **ones** whom thy great virtues
    shame.

XXI.

The storm rules for the night; but in the **morn**
Cometh tranquility. The winds are low,
And clouds have sunk to rest, and there is born
A thing **of** heavenly beauty, which doth show
The power that rules the storm. 'Tis the bright bow
That God hath set i' th' heavens; the changing light
Which, like a bending angel, sheds a glow
Of calm, and tranquil beauty o'er the bright
And joyous earth, redeemed from storm and tempest's
    night.

XXII.

And now, safe anchored near the **destined port,**
The fleet collected stands.   On either hand,
On each opposing shore, a frowning fort
Rises majestic, and their guns command
The harbor and its entrance.   On the land,
Exulting as the hunter o'er his prey,
The foe watch for our coming, as our **band**
'**Moves fearless on,** the Wabash leads **the way,**
The others follow her in battle's **firm array.**

XXIII.

Upon that autumn morn there was revealed
A scene of terrible grandeur, **such as earth**
Reveals but rarely.   Rarely doth she yield
Monsters of such sublimity.   '**Twere** worth
A life of common things, 'mid the world's dearth
Of stirring scenes, to see this day.   **His eyes,**
Who of **these imps of time beholds the birth,**
Are blest indeed, and the dissolving skies,
And earth by fire consumed **shall scarcely cause sur-**
              prise.

XXIV.

Now o'er the nearer fort a wreath of smoke
Curls, and the cannon's roar gives to the fleet
A soldier's welcome, which, as soon as spoke,
Is answered warmly, and the vessels greet
The foe with fiery ardor.   They repeat
Again with equal warmth.   From either shore
Now comes the greeting, and the ships compete
In compliments with each.   A deafening roar
Succeeds, while o'er the scene the clouds of battle
     lower,

XXV.

And hide its sickening myst'ries.   It were well
Could they be hid forever.   Earth, thank God,
Hath few such horrors, and the fiery hell
Presents few scenes more terrible.   The rod
With which the prophet hatched th' accursed brood
Of darkness, plagues, and fire, had not the power
For deadly evil, of man's unsubdued,
Dark, and revengeful passions, the curst dower
Bestowed when reason led him to her nuptial bower.

XXVI.

Upon the wave, a storm of shot, and shell,
Of crashing timbers, and of falling masts,
And fires which the engulfing wave shall quell,
Whelming also their victims; while the blasts
O' th' cannon's mouth, seem those volcano casts
From the high crater, when his molten waves
Pour from the trembling earth; and Death, while
     lasts
The storm above, and the hoarse battle raves,
Gathers his victims down unto their watery graves.

XXVII.

Upon the land, a rain of leaden hail
Falling from sulph'rous clouds: while bursting shells,
Scatt'ring destruction, make the bravest quail,
And bursts upon the ear the cry that tells
Of mortal suffering, as the dread shower quells
The fires of life. Now each embattled tower
Rocks from its base, as the dark storm dispels
Its boasted strength, and, falling in a shower
Of crumbling stone, it doth its inmates overpower.

XXVIII.

And overpowered they fly.   Their serpent flag
Trails in its native element, the dust,
Hurled from the ramparts.   The survivors lag
Not for the landing of the fleet ; but trust
Distance, for safety from the storm which must
O'erwhelm them should they stay.   That **fatal day**
Showed them the power a nation may entrust
To " Neptune's minions," when they dare essay
Their strength 'gainst **walls of stone in battles equal
fray.**

XXIX.

The strife is over, and the murky cloud
That hid its mysteries, passing **away,**
Reveals the fleet lying at anchor proud,
The undisputed master of the bay
And its defenses: **and the God of Day,**
Sinking in splendor **'neath the western sea,**
Beholds the colors that have won the fray,
Floating from masts and towers triumphantly,
The gallant stars and stripes, the flag of Liberty.

XXX.

Hail Banner of the Free!   The meteor bright,
Whose advent glad dispelled the sickening dearth
Of freedom's hope from tyranny's dark night,
And, shining splendid, prophesied the birth
Of that Republic, whose redeeming worth
Lived in the statesman's hope, the poet's dream,
And turned to actual shape, exists on earth,
A blest reality! and whose bright gleam
Has guided since its course upon time's changing
    stream.

XXXI.

Our fathers followed thy unchanging light,
Through the dark time which history endears;
By day their pillar, and their fire by night,
Thou ledst them through the wilderness of tears,
Suffering, and blood, that marked the rising years
Of the Republic's star: and, when she rose,
Triumphant o'er the vapors of their fears;
Thee, for her guardian and her guide, they chose,
A comfort to her friends, a terror to her foes.

XXXII.

Emblem of Liberty !   When gentle peace
Reigns calm and tranquil o'er the happy land;
While yields the lab'ring earth her glad increase,
And plenteous gold rewards the workman's hand,
Thy brilliant folds, by whispering zephyrs fanned,
Grace the bright pageant of some gala day,
Or float majestic from the turrets grand
Of stately capitols, or, flaunting gay,
Bedeck our ships of trade in many a peaceful bay.

XXXIII.

Terror of Tyranny !   When war's loud blasts
Sound o'er the shuddering land, and thou art whirled
Aloft on battle's winds; while God recasts
Earth's dynasties and kingdoms, and are hurled
The bolts that rend the nations : then unfurled
Thou rid'st war's tempest, the avenger bright,
But terrible, who, 'gainst th' embattled world,
Maintains the flame of Freedom's sacred light
Triumphant o'er the gloom of slavery's dark night !

XXXIV.

Flag of a country's hope, a nation's pride !
Thine every emblem speaks of Liberty:
Thy red the patriotic blood that dyed
Thy sheltering folds, when those who would be free,
Sought in the skies, thy natvie blue which be,
Freedom not found on earth. Thy spotless white
Implies thy first unsullied purity ;
Thy stripes scourge freedom's foes, and, glitt'ring
    bright,
Thy stars shall guide her way through war's uncer-
    tain night.

XXXV.

And thou shalt wave forever: when the earth,
Fruitful from thine embrace, in future days,
Her labors past, rejoices in the birth
Of universal freedom ; then her praise
Shall be to thee, the father, as her gaze
Joys in the beauty of the child ; and time
Shall still increase thine honors ; the sun's rays
Ne'er set on thy wide regions, and each clime
Shall own thy mighty power, thy majesty sublime.

XXXVI.

There won Dupont unfading laurels; there
To its zenith rose the light of Sherman's fame,
Which, with a brightness time may not impair,
Far shining through the years, shall make his name
A star in the nation's heaven: they may claim
Undying honors both.   By sea and land
They bore their country's flag, their zeal the same;
'Mid danger's waves, and on war's treach'rous sand,
Our anchor, and our shield, their sacred names shall
     stand.

XXXVII.

Upon that day, in hostile ranks arrayed,
Two brothers, leaders both, waged deadly strife
Against each other, and their power essayed
In all its force, each 'gainst the other's life.
Had war's hard mandate bid them take the knife,
And dare the combat close; had they obeyed
And plunged the steel? God knows: war's scenes
     are rife
With kindred horrors, whose dread forms displayed,
In gloom and darkness might eclipse hell's blackest
    shade.

XXXVIII.

In the bright spring time of their boyhood's hours,
Their little barks upon life's laughing waves
Had danced together, careless of the showers
Which autumn brings, and the hoarse storm that
    raves
Through life's most dreary winter, e'er the grave's
Protecting walls have broke its chilling powers.
Their summer sun saw them the willing slaves
Of interest's winds. Now, while war's storm cloud
    lowers,
They ride opposing waves, and dwell in hostile towers.

XXXIX.

Mistaken they who deem affection's chains
Powerful to bind through life th' unbroken band
Of lasting friendship. The cold heart disdains
The tender tie: ambition's stern demand;
Or sordid avarice with his griping hand,
Shatter its links: although our youthful veins
Beat warm, and high, with the pulsation grand
Of human love; too soon their ardor wanes,
And o'er our latter years, cold, selfish interest reigns.

XL.

Where are the loved companions of thy youth,
Those with thine early joys and sorrows blended?
Whose firm love, and unalterable truth,
Had any questioned thou hadst been offended:
Hadst thou, to-day, the need to be befriended,
Wouldst thou, the denizen of some humble booth,
Enter on friendship's steps their palace splendid;
Or would their slaves, with mingled wrath and ruth,
Spurn from their gilded doors thy rustic form un-
      couth?

XLI.

Happy is he, who from life's sparkling chalice
Ne'er quaffed the dregs of dread reality;
Nor saw at once his sand-enfounded palace
Stripped by the mad waves of fatality
Of its high semblance of regality,
And by the blasts of envy, hate, and malice,
In ruin hurled to its finality;
And whose untutored eye has not grown callous
To the false gleam of life's auroraborealis.

LXII.

Earth is a market place, where human souls
Are current coin for pleasure, power and gold,
Man's greatest needs: the vendress, Fate, controls
The price and quantity, and doth unfold
Her tempting wares, gaining herself untold,
Unknown advantages: the food she doles
Being the buyer's poison; he hath sold
Himself to her dread wiles; his head soon rolls
'Neath her dissevering ax, his body feeds the ghouls:

XLIII.

This is why men of lofty minds, have found
Companionship in lonely solitudes,
And felt the sweetest discourse to abound
Where the dread silence everlasting broods;
The moisture which from some lone rock exudes,
Has been the inspiring wine that did compound
Their most exalted fancies. The green woods
Have their high brows with fadeless laurels crowned,
And earth's dread mysteries to their high fame re-
        dound.

XLIV.*

He who, from the soul-chilling eminence
Of earthly pomp and circumstance descending;
In the rough garb of native innocence,
Seeks the lone shrine, where nature's vestals blending
Their ceaseless prayers, feed the slow flame unending
Before her altar; sees the evidence
Of her high power, and, on thought's steps ascending,
Enters her holy place with confidence,
And read th' unwritten book, and, to his spirit's
    sense,

XLV.

Silence hath many voices, and the waste
Of barren deserts drear is rife with seeds
Of wisdom's fadeless tree; and he shall taste
In riper years its fruits; and, as he feeds,
The blood that prompts high tho'ts and noble deeds
Shall, through his swelling veins, coursing in haste,
Bear godlike power. The arid sand that breeds
To others thirst and death, by him embraced,
Brings forth springs of exhaustless thought, and the
    high placed,

XLVI.

And light crowned daughters of the regal night
Come near to him, and pour into his soul
The care destroying, hope inspiring light
Of love and sympathy : to him, the whole
Arcana of the universe is but the scroll
Of man's high destiny, and from the height,
And depth of infinite space, he hears the roll
Of nature's pealing organ, and its might
Subdues his soul to harmony.   If heard aright,

XLVII.

The sea's fond plaint to the repellant shore :
The myriad voices that from trees and plants
Whisper their infinite yearnings : tempests roar ;
The changing cries each living creature grants,
Are but the solemn hymn which nature chants,
Through all the rolling years.   Blended, they pour
Forth the great symphony, whose grandeur haunts
The soul in dreams, and to our inmost core
Thrills the grand mystery of earth's divinest lore.

XLVIII.

This is the anthem which the spirit hears,
When, by the path of dreams, she seeks the bowers.
In the bright gardens of the future years,
Where radiant Psyche culls thought's rarest flowers
To deck faith's nuptial chambers, in the towers
Where reason reigns: Its harmony endears
All things of which it breathes, and overpowers
The passions with a sacred joy that cheers
The soul, too deep for mirth, too purely blest for tears.

XLIX.

And there shall come a time, when every ear
Shall be attuned to this blest harmony:
When the glad millions of the rescued sphere
Shall make the notes of the great symphony
The music of their worship.   It shall be
When superstition, tyranny, and fear,
Are driven from the earth; and liberty,
And reason reign supreme.   Then shall appear
The time of rest foretold by many a visioned seer.

L.

Swift pass the years, in sorrow and in pain,
Driven like chaff before time's breath away:
The pregnant grains of wisdom's seed remain:
The mists of error fade before the ray
That tells the dawn of truth's resplendent day:
The shattered links of slavery's galling chain,
Sunk in Time's depths, are not less lost than they;
And Truth and Freedom, with their blended train,
Come on the car of Time, o'er the glad earth to reign.

CANTO FOURTH.

I.

Up the swift Cumberland I see advancing
A well-manned fleet to join **the deadly strife,**
Swift and impatient on the blue **wave dancing,**
It walks the waters like a thing of life;
While on its swarming decks the drum and fife
Discourse the stirring notes whose power dispels
All thoughts of fear, and whose deep tones are rife
With the **subduing melody which swells**
Up **from the heart, and every thought of danger quells.**

II.

Now, in its most exalted notes uprising,
It wafts the spirit to a purer sphere;
Now, with a plaintive sadness realizing
All that our love and reverence hold most **dear,**
It claims for them the homage of **a tear:**
Now the hoarse drum breaks **in, the cymbals clash,**
And the loud trumpet speaks unto the ear
Its soul inspiring notes: their blended crash
Dispels all tender **thoughts, and substitutes a rash,**

III.

Unthinking, reckless courage, 'neath whose spell,
As the doomed serpent, at the mystic notes
Of the weird charmer, leaves his quiet cell,
Seeking the strain whose dim remembrance floats
Down from the fabled past, and, as he gloats,
Forgets the wily singer's feudal hate ;
To mortal ears, the cannon's brazen throats
Pour fourth sweet melody, which doth create
A senseless bravery defying death and fate.

IV.

Such is the scene on the upper decks: below,
From out the portholes frown in silent scorn,
With the calm, patient gaze of those, who know
Their power, and bide their time, yet inly mourn
From out their quiet haven to be torn,
And cast adrift upon life's stormy ocean,
The guns in whose mysterious depths are borne,
Held by the charm of some spell-bearing potion,
The sleeping elements which, wakened into motion,

v.

Shall tell the awe-struck earth the mighty power
Which sleeps sublime within their pulseless veins,
As the deep-moated wall, and firm-set tower,
The marts of trade, and the high-reaching fanes
Whose every spire the sordid earth disdains,
Trembling with terror at their voice deep-booming,
Are hurled in ruins toward their native plains,
In stately pride their human lords entombing,
While the black cloud of war, its hideous form up-
    looming,

vi.

Seems the reality which doth arise,
A hollow form above hope's scattered ashes,
Where our fond eyes beheld a glorious prize
Lit by our fancy's never-resting flashes
Into a thing of beauty; won, it dashes
Away our cup of happiness forever;
While the applause which greets our conquest, clashes
Discordant, on a spirit which shall never
Own more th' ennobling power of its first high en-
    deavor.

VII.

A cheer, a flash, the cannon's boom defying
The fleet's advance, now greets it from the shore :
A flash, a trembling, as its guns replying
From out their brazen mouths in anger pour
Their well aimed shot, and join the stunning roar ;
Now the quick eye discerns the glittering track
Where the swift fire-winged shells loud-whizzing soar
To rend their prey, and loudly answer back
The battle's thunder from the war cloud's shifting
    rack.

VIII.

Swift play the boatmen's guns ; but swifter come
The crashing missiles of the vengeful foe,
And still the screaming fife, and sullen drum
Send forth their notes above, and still below,
Where the hot furnaces with anger glow,
The gunners ply their busy task, and loud
The guns belch forth defiance as they throw
The deadly shot ; while spreads the battle's cloud
A shield for those who live, and for the dead a
    shroud.

IX.

I see adown the Cumberland descending,
Broken and helpless, on the drifting flood,
A scattered fleet, and with the waters blending,
From off its dripping decks, the hues of blood;
While many a manly form, which proudly stood
A tower of strength against th' insulting foe,
Lies shattered, mute, and motionless; subdued,
And silent, never shall they **know**
Again the battle's call, or feel th' inspiring **glow**

X.

Of martial courage, as the bugle's note
Sends the warm blood swift **coursing through their**
     veins;
But down death's silent waters they shall float,
To join the tenants of those peopled plains
Where endless rest in peace and silence reigns;
While far above the battle's misty shroud,
Freed **from th'** influence of their earthly stains,
Their souls, with more than mortal powers endowed,
Shall **seek** the land of light which lies beyond the
     cloud.

XI.

Above the fleet, unmindful of the slaughters
Whose gory drops, the hues of life bestowing,
Shall mingle with the gladness of its waters
A tinge of crime, and to their waves unknowing
Before the dreadful secret, baneful glowing,
Shall tell the tale of life, and the dark lore
Of wrong, revenge, and death; clear, and swift flow-
    ing,
The river's tides their tribute downward pour
Betwixt its prisoning banks, and, blending with their
    roar,

XII.

I hear a rustling 'mid the yellow blades
Which crown the fields through which its waters sweep,
And, quick advancing through the woods and glades
Which skirt the banks along its western steep,
The tread of armed men. Come they to reap?
Yes! and for whom? For Death, the master dread!
The fleecy tears the pitying skies now weep
Spread over earth an ermine robe, which red
Shall be with human blood in deadly conflict shed.

XIII.

I see the field toward which they take their way,
Sloping aback from yonder bluff which stands
As sent'nel o'er the stream, and men in gray
Cast up the loosened earth with busy hands.
Is the soil fruitful?   Yes! these warring bands
Shall yield a harvest here whose increase great
Might satisfy their master's full demands
For many a year to come, if aught could sate
That all devouring churl, the minister of Fate.

XIV.

There comes a whisper on the wand'ring winds
Which kiss the laughing waves of Cumberland.
Is it the murmur of the storm that finds
Its place of rest in some far distant land?
No! but a deadlier storm shall take its stand,
And lash these shudd'ring banks with its dread
      power;
But its emotive sprites shall it remand
To whence it came; while falls the battle's shower
Swift and unpitying through many a weary hour.

XV.

I hear a scream, a crash, a deaf'ning roar,
Upon the western banks of Cumberland:
I see the men in gray in fury pour
Down from the embattled height, and, hand to hand,
They meet the men in blue, and, as each band
Falls back for respite short, a crimson wave
Changes the hue of the dividing land
O'er which again, to conquest or a grave,
They rush, while war's hoarse storms with double
     fury rave.

XVI.

I see the blue retire before the gray,
And both in battle's smoke almost concealed:
Now they stand firm, and now the equal fray
Rages with double fury, as they wield
Their fullest power, and either scorns to yield,
While each with equal hate the other spurns,
When Grant, long-wished, appears upon the field:
His practised eye each vital point discerns;
His skillful courage soon the tide of battle turns.

He rallies to its post our broken right:
He charges with our left the rebel lines:
Directs each movement of the shifting fight,
And in each change his practised eye defines
Among the foe, he skillfully divines
The object of their movement, and with swift,
And mathematic certainty combines
Our well arranged battalions, quick to shift
    Their course where battle's clouds their blackest
        forms uplift.

XVIII

Brave Wallace now with desperate valor charges:
And now McClernand joins the welcome fray:
Now, as our courage with our strength enlarges,
Our cheers of loud defiance spread dismay
Among the enemy, and the quick play
Of the swift rolling deadly cannon balls
Scatters them right and left, and wins the day;
Their discomfited army backward falls,
    And seeks with eager haste the fort's protecting walls.

XIX.

Next morn upon the Sabbath air outfloated
Above Fort Donelson a flag of white,
The preconcerted signal which denoted
The enemy's surrender: E'er the night
Our forces held the long contested height,
And eager groups about the campfires told
The stirring scenes and ventures of the fight,
Sang the loud praises of their leaders bold,
And the heroic dead lamented and extolled.

XX.

There rose the star which in the latter years,
Above the clouds of battle mounting high,
Outshone the galaxy of its compeers,
And beamed triumphant in the nation's sky,
A thing of mighty power and majesty,
Before whose steady brilliance treason's light,
Faded and waned, until, about to die,
Too weak to dare the contest, scorning flight,
Its captive vot'ries swelled the measure of its
    might.

XXI.

Till with the brilliance of its native worth
The bright renown of conquered chiefs was blended,
And the proud honors which a grateful North
To the brave champions of her rights extended,
Made by their centered power a vision splendid,
Which to fame's starry heaven's high confines
Above the mists of calumny ascended,
And, in the sphere which merit's law assigns,
A fixed, and changeless light with treble brilliance
    shines.

XXII.

Long as the story of our bitter wrongs
Nobly avenged, our vindicated rights,
Is told to earth, and history prolongs
The stirring record of our bloody fights,
And the full canvass shows their moving sights,
While a free people to a fruitful land
The wanderer of every clime invites,
Linked with each action of the contest grand,
Loved, honored, **and** revered, the name of Grant shall
    stand.

XXIII.

Thus have I woven into idle song
The thronging mem'ries of eventful days;
Should you approve th' attempt, I may prolong
In future time the theme, and to your gaze
Present the scenes whose recollection weighs
Upon my waking hours, and midnight dreams,
A vision ever present, a wild maze
Of battles, sails, and marches, wherein gleams
Truth's light, and Freedom's star with steady bril-
  liance beams.

XXIV.

If you approve it not, why then, farewell,
And let this ill-judged trial be my last,
And I will strive to break the powerful spell
Which conjures up these visions of the past.
But that the mind's horizon is o'ercast
With common forms, and shapes of earthy mold,
Then might the thrilling story of the vast
And gorgeous imagery, which doth unfold
Itself to the soul's gaze, be well and truly told.

XXV.

The mind sees clearly ; the soul's subtle fires
Glow with a beauty which is not of earth,
And the imprisoned spirit still aspires
Toward the heritage of its high birth ;
But our dull clay obscures their native worth,
And damps their ardor, and expression tires
To body forth their feelings from the dearth
Of words adapted to their high desires,
And lists their notes in vain from the world's grand-
    est lyres.

XXVI.

If, in the future years, a bard shall rise,
Of purpose pure, in aspiration high,
Noble and good, benevolent and wise,
To whom the earth and air, the sea and sky,
Shall be as things familiar, and whose eye
Shall pierce the mists of human doubts and fears,
He shall pour forth a song, whose melody
Shall float unbroken down the tide of years,
And mingle with the crash of the dissolving spheres.

XXVII.

Till then our waiting souls must be content,
Amid the darkness of our mental night,
To watch the fitful flashes which are sent
Athwart the firmament's englooming might.
As he, who with the candle's flick'ring light
Supplies the place of the resplendent day ;
We wait the destined bard, who from our sight
Shall roll the weight of error's stone away,
And flood the waiting earth with Truth's eternal
    ray.